# 50 Fill-In Math Word Problems

## FRACTIONS & DECIMALS

### Grades 4–6

by Bob Krech and Joan Novelli

New York • Toronto • London • Auckland • Sydney
Mexico City • New Delhi • Hong Kong • Buenos Aires

**Teaching** *Resources*

Thanks to Andrew and Faith for laughing

Editor: Joan Novelli
Cover design by Jason Robinson
Interior design by Holly Grundon
Interior illustrations by Mike Moran

ISBN-13: 978-0-545-07486-5
ISBN-10: 0-545-07486-X

# Contents

## Fill-In Math Word Problems

# About This Book

When we learn to read, we learn to recognize the letters of the alphabet, we practice letter-sound relationships, and we learn punctuation, but what it's all about is eventually being able to read text. A similar situation exists in math. We learn how to recognize and write numerals, what the symbols mean, and we learn operations such as multiplication and division, but what it's all about is what you can do with these skills—applying what you know to solve problems. *50 Fill-In Math Word Problems: Fractions & Decimals* provides lots of funny stories to fill in—and some very interesting problems to solve.

## What Are Fill-In Math Word Problems?

A fill-in math word problem is a funny story with a math problem waiting to happen. Most of the word problem is already supplied except for a few key words and numbers that have been removed and replaced with blanks. It's up to the students to fill in those blanks with missing nouns, verbs, adjectives, and other types of words—just like in some other popular word games. The difference is that this game is missing some numbers as well. When your students supply the missing numbers along with the words, they suddenly have a wacky, math word problem that's fun to read and solve!

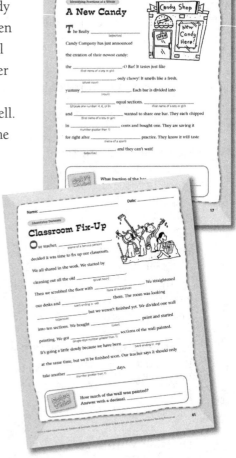

## Why Use Fill-In Math Word Problems?

Traditional math word problems can provide a meaningful context for students to apply their skills, but sometimes the problems can be a bit boring. Remember trying to figure out when the two trains would pass each other? That won't happen with *50 Fill-In Math Word Problems*. Students help create these wacky word problems, which provide for plenty of good problem-solving practice with grade-appropriate math skills and concepts. Have fun while doing math? Absolutely!

# Teaching With Fill-In Math Word Problems

The stories in this book are organized by skill level, beginning with those that provide practice with fractions, followed by decimals. You can choose a fill-in story to use with the entire class, or select as many as needed to match different ability levels of students. For example, you might have some students who would benefit from practice with multiplying fractions, while others may need more time with addition with fractions. (For connections to the math standards, see Meeting the Math Standards, page 12.) Whatever the need, there is a set of fill-in stories to support it. Following is the order of stories by skills.

- Identifying Fractions of a Whole
- Identifying Fractions of a Set
- Comparing Fractions of a Whole
- Comparing Fractions of a Set
- Addition With Fractions
- Subtraction With Fractions
- Multiplication With Fractions

- Division With Fractions
- Identifying Decimals
- Comparing Decimals
- Addition With Decimals
- Subtraction With Decimals
- Multiplication With Decimals
- Division With Decimals

## Teaching Tips

When teaching with the stories in this book, be sure to review and reinforce the following strategies with students.

- Use commas in numbers with four or more digits to keep all those digits organized.

- When comparing numbers—for example, to see which one is greater—write down the numbers one on top of the other, with the digits aligned, in order to make an accurate visual comparison. When working with decimals that do not have the same number of digits, such as 0.32 and 0.299, it is a good idea to add a zero or zeros to the end of the number with fewer digits so that the comparison is clear. In this case, we could change 0.32 to 0.320, so students would be able to line up the two numbers and compare each place value easily.

- When performing operations (addition, subtraction, multiplication, and division), align digits and decimals properly to avoid mistakes in computation.

- It is almost always easier to do comparisons and computations with fractions when they have like denominators. Encourage students to use multiplication or division to change fractions accordingly. For example, when comparing $1/3$ and $1/4$, we could multiply the fractions so that each has a denominator of 12. The result would be $4/12$ and $3/12$. It is a much clearer comparison now.

- When solving equations, check the final answer and ask yourself if it makes sense. To do a number-sense check, round the numbers in question to get a reasonable estimate of what the answer should be. This provides a point of comparison to determine whether the actual answer does indeed make sense. (For more problem-solving strategies, see Teaching Problem-Solving Skills: The Fantastic Five-Step Process, page 9.)

## Modeling the Process

Before expecting students to complete stories on their own, model the process of filling in the blanks for a story and solving the problem. Use an overhead to project the story so students can follow along. Invite a student to help you out, and follow these steps:

**1.** Starting at the beginning of the story, read the prompts for the fill-ins—for example, "verb ending in *-ing*." Write in the verb your helper suggests—for example, *shrinking*.

**2.** When you have filled in all of the blanks, read aloud the story, beginning with the title.

**3.** Read aloud the problem in "Solve This!" and think aloud as you use information from the story to solve the problem. (This is a good time to model how to use the Fantastic Five-Step Process. See page 9 for more information.)

## How to Fill in the Blanks

Each fill-in math word problem requires students to fill in a set of words and numbers to complete the story. They will then use some of the information they provide to solve the problem. Following is more detailed information about how to fill in the blanks.

### Choosing Words

From singular and plural nouns to adverbs and exclamations, different kinds of words are required to fill in the blanks of fill-in math word problems. Review each type of word with students, using the Word Choice Chart (page 13) as a guide. To help students create their own handy references, have them complete the third column of their chart with additional examples of each type of fill-in. They can refer to this when completing stories as a reminder of what kinds of words they can use. You might also consider transferring the descriptions and examples to a wall chart for easy reference.

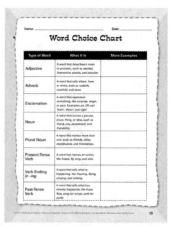

Note that, at times, students will also have to fill in some other types of words, such as a color, the name of a place, or a letter of the alphabet. These are not included in the chart, as these prompts are already specific enough to support students in their word choice. When you introduce any new story to students, just take a moment to review the different types of words that will be required.

## Choosing Numbers

Many stories include fill-ins that give students choice within a range, such as "number between 6 and 19." Some fill-ins are more open-ended—for example, "number greater than 1." Other stories may be more specific about the number choice—for example, a fill-in for "Birthday Cake" (page 31) requires students to "choose a number: 2, 3, or 4." You may choose to let students fill in numbers according to the directions in the stories as is, or you can modify the parameters to provide for differentiation of instruction, individualizing the problems for students by using the number ranges that make sense for them. If you do change the fill-in prompts in this way, be sure to check for other numbers in the story that may also need to be changed. However, keep in mind that leaving the number size open-ended to some extent is an interesting option, and will provide information as to students' ability to work with different-size numbers.

## Lesson Formats

There are many ways to use the stories in *50 Fill-In Math Word Problems* in your classroom. Suggested lesson formats follow.

### 1. Problem-Solving Partners

Have students pair up. Make copies of a fill-in story and distribute to one student in each pair. These students are the Readers. Without revealing the title or any parts of the story itself, Readers ask their partners for the missing words and numbers in order ("plural noun," "adjective," "single-digit number greater than 1," and so on) and fill in the appropriate blanks with their partner's responses. When all the blanks are filled in, the Reader reads the completed story. The resulting silly story now contains a math word problem! Partners solve the problem (together or independently), sharing strategies and checking their answers.

### 2. Class Stories

Choose a story and let students take turns supplying words and numbers to fill in the blanks (again, just read the fill-in prompts in turn, but do not reveal the story at this point). When the story is complete, read it to the class. Have students take notes on the numbers in the story and the problem they need to solve. (Or write this information on chart paper for them.) Students can work together as a class, with a partner, or independently to solve the problem. As a follow-up, let students share answers and discuss problem-solving strategies.

### 3. Story Switcheroo

After students fill in the blanks for a story with a partner, make copies and distribute to the class for extra practice or homework. Twenty different versions of one story mean 20 different problems to solve! And students will love seeing their work used as a teaching tool!

### 4. Math Practice Pages

Invite pairs of students to create stories for a binder full of practice pages. They fill in the stories as for "Problem-Solving Partners" (see page 7), but write the answer and an explanation on the back of the paper. For extra practice, students can take a story from the binder, solve the problem (on a separate sheet of paper), and check their answer on the back. They can then return the story to the binder.

### 5. Create New Stories

Creating new fill-in stories is another option for practicing math skills—and a motivating way to connect writing and math. Using the stories in this book as models, invite students to write their own wacky, fill-in math stories. With students' permission, copy the stories and distribute to the class for homework (or in-class practice). Guide students in following these steps to create their stories.

- Identify a skill area and write this at the top of the paper. You may choose to specify a skill area for students, such as "Multiplying Fractions," or leave this up to students to decide.

- Brainstorm story ideas. Everyday events, such as getting ready for school or sharing a snack, can make for very funny stories. Think about how fractions and decimals might fit into the story. For example, anytime something is shared there is going to be a fraction. So if three friends are sharing a candy bar equally, they will want to know what part, or what fraction of the whole candy bar, they each get.

- Write a draft of your story. Do not try to make your story "funny." Just write about the event as if you were telling someone else about it. When you're finished, underline some of the verbs, adjectives, nouns, and numbers, then erase the original word. Label the type of word or number beneath each blank. Be sure to set up a math problem in the story.

- Write the problem to be solved in the space labeled "Solve This!" Solve the problem yourself to make sure it works.

- Draw a picture to illustrate the story.

**Teaching Problem-Solving Skills:**

# The Fantastic Five-Step Process

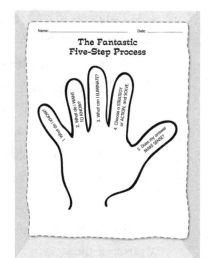

Problem solving is the first process standard listed in the National Council of Teachers Mathematics (NCTM) *Principles and Standards for Mathematics*. The accompanying statement reads, "Problem solving is an integral part of all mathematics learning. In everyday life and in the workplace, being able to solve problems can lead to great advantages. However, solving problems is not only a goal of learning mathematics but also a major means of doing so. Problem solving should not be an isolated part of the curriculum but should involve all Content Standards." In other words, in mathematics, problem solving is what it's all about!

What do you do when you first encounter a math word problem? This is what we need to help students deal with. We need to help them develop a process that they can use effectively to solve any type of math word problem. Word problems often intimidate students because there may be a lot of information, the information is embedded in text, and unlike a regular equation, it is not always clear exactly what you are supposed to do. When using these fill-in math word problems, you may want to take some time to teach (and subsequently review) the Fantastic Five-Step Process for problem solving.

The Fantastic Five-Step Process helps students approach problem solving in a logical, systematic way. No matter what type of problem students encounter, these five steps will help them through it. Learning and using the five steps will help students organize their interpretation and thinking about the problem. This is the key to good problem solving—organizing for action. The best way to help students understand the process is to demonstrate it as you work through a problem on the whiteboard or overhead. Make a copy of the graphic organizer on page 14. You can enlarge this to poster size or provide students with individual copies to follow along as you take them through an introductory lesson.

## Step 1: What Do I Know?

Begin by writing the following problem on the board or overhead: *Cal's fifth-grade class is celebrating the opening day of baseball season with a hotdog party. There are 20 students altogether. When the teacher asked what they wanted on their hotdogs, five said ketchup, five said mustard, three said relish, two said onions, and five said both ketchup and mustard. What fraction of the class wants relish or onions only?*

Ask students to read the problem carefully. Ask: "What are the facts?" Have students volunteer these orally. Write them on the board—for example:

- Cal is in fifth grade.
- Cal's class is having a hotdog party to celebrate the opening day of baseball season.
- There are 20 students in the class.
- Five kids want ketchup only.
- Five kids want mustard only.
- Three kids want relish only.
- Two kids want onions only.
- Five kids want ketchup and mustard together.

Encourage students to write down the facts themselves, too. This will help them focus on what's important while looking for ways to put it in a more accessible form. Ask: "Can we arrange the facts in a way that will help us understand the problem?" For example, it might be good to draw what we know, or put it in a list, or make a table. Sometimes it's helpful to arrange numbers from lower to higher or higher to lower, especially when making comparisons. Using letters to abbreviate the toppings can help us construct a simple, easy-to-read table. This is a good way to "break out" the facts and make them clear.

| K = ketchup  M = mustard  R = relish  O = onions | | | | | | |
|---|---|---|---|---|---|---|
| Topping | K | M | R | O | K & M | |
| # of Students | 5 | 5 | 3 | 2 | 5 | = 20 students |

## Step 2: What Do I Want to Know?

What is the question in the problem? What are we trying to find out? It's a good idea to have students state the question and also determine how the answer will be labeled. For example if the answer is 15, 15 what? 15 pizzas? 15 pennies? In this problem we want to know what fraction of the class wants relish or onions only, so we know that answer will be labeled "of the class."

## Step 3: What Can I Eliminate?

Once we know what we are trying to find out, we can decide what is unimportant. You may need all the information, but often enough there is extra information that can be put aside to help focus on the facts. For example, we can eliminate the fact that Cal is in fifth grade and that his class is having a party.

We're left with the following:

- There are 20 students in the class.
- Five kids want ketchup only.
- Five kids want mustard only.
- Three kids want relish only.
- Two kids want onions only.
- Five kids want ketchup and mustard together, but no relish or onions.

## Step 4: Choose a Strategy or Action and Solve.

Is there an action in the story—for example, is something being "taken away" or is something being "added" that will help us decide on an operation or a way to solve the problem? We have to find out how many kids want only relish or onions. We know how many want each of those, but what part of the class is that? If we look at our table and remember we are trying to express our answer as a fraction, we can look at all of our data in terms of fractions.

| K = ketchup  M = mustard  R = relish  O = onions | | | | | |
|---|---|---|---|---|---|
| Topping | K | M | R | O | K & M |  |
| # of Students | $\frac{5}{20}$ | $\frac{5}{20}$ | $\frac{3}{20}$ | $\frac{2}{20}$ | $\frac{5}{20}$ | = 20 students |

We see that $2/20$ of the class wanted onions only and $3/20$ wanted relish only. If we add these two fractions together, $2/20 + 3/20$, we get $5/20$. If we reduce $5/20$, our answer will be $1/4$. So we could say $1/4$ of the class wanted relish or onions only.

## Step 5: Does My Answer Make Sense?

Reread the problem. Look at the answer. Is it reasonable? Is it a sensible answer given what we know? The answer does make sense. We see that if we add $2/20$ and $3/20$ and get $5/20$, or $1/4$, in comparison to the other toppings it is exactly the same amount, and so it is 1 of 4 equal amounts or $1/4$. If we add up the amounts we would get $20/20$ or 1 whole, otherwise known as the entire class. This makes sense, also. Try a couple of sample word problems using this "talk-through" format with students. You might invite students to try the problem themselves first and then review step-by-step together, sharing solutions to see if all steps were considered and solutions are in fact correct. Practicing the process in this way helps make it part of a student's way of thinking mathematically.

**Teaching Tip**

Note that there are no answer keys for the fill-in math word problems as answers will vary depending on the numbers students supply to fill in the blanks. You might set up a buddy system for checking answers or have students turn in their stories for you to check. The fill-in stories provide good opportunities to reinforce strategies for determining if an answer is reasonable.

# Meeting the Math Standards

The fill-in math word problems in this book include math content designed to support you in meeting the following math standards for number and operations across grades 4–6, as outlined by the National Council of Teachers of Mathematics (NCTM) in *Principles and Standards for School Mathematics*.

## Understand numbers, ways of representing numbers, relationships among numbers, and number systems

- understand the place-value structure of the base-ten number system and be able to represent and compare whole numbers and decimals
- recognize equivalent representations for the same number and generate them by decomposing and composing numbers
- develop understanding of fractions as parts of unit wholes, as parts of a collection, as locations on number lines, and as divisions of whole numbers
- use models, benchmarks, and equivalent forms to judge the size of fractions
- recognize and generate equivalent forms of commonly used fractions, decimals, and percents
- describe classes of numbers according to characteristics such as the nature of their factors
- use fractions and decimals to solve problems

## Understand meanings of operations and how they relate to one another

- understand various meanings of multiplication and division
- understand the effects of multiplying and dividing whole numbers
- identify and use relationships between operations, such as division as the inverse of multiplication, to solve problems
- understand and use properties of operations, such as the distributivity of multiplication over addition
- understand and use arithmetic operations with fractions and decimals
- simplify computations with integers, fractions, and decimals

## Compute fluently and make reasonable estimates

- develop fluency with basic number combinations for multiplication and division and use these combinations to mentally compute related problems

- develop fluency in adding, subtracting, multiplying, and dividing whole numbers
- develop and use strategies to estimate the results of whole-number computations and to judge the reasonableness of such results
- use visual models, benchmarks, and equivalent forms to add and subtract commonly used fractions and decimals
- select appropriate methods and tools for computing (whole numbers, fractions, and decimals) from among mental computation, estimation, calculators, and paper and pencil

## The word problems in this book also support the NCTM process standards as follows:

### Problem Solving

- solve problems that arise in mathematics and other contexts
- apply and adapt a variety of appropriate strategies to solve problems

### Reasoning and Proof

- select and use various types of reasoning and methods of proof

### Communication

- communicate mathematical thinking coherently and clearly

### Connections

- understand how mathematical ideas interconnect and build on one another
- recognize and apply mathematics in contexts outside of mathematics

### Representation

- create and use representations to organize, record, and communicate mathematical ideas
- use representations to model and interpret physical, social, and mathematical phenomena

Source: *Principles and Standards for School Mathematics* (National Council of Teachers of Mathematics, 2000-2004); www.standards.nctm.org.

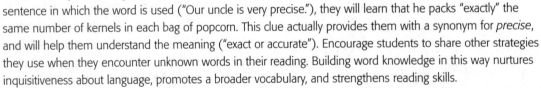

Take advantage of vocabulary-building opportunities that these fill-in stories present. For example, in the story "Our Uncle's Popcorn" (page 19), students will encounter the word *precise*. Use words such as this to reinforce word recognition strategies. In this case, context provides a good clue to the meaning of *precise*. If students read past the sentence in which the word is used ("Our uncle is very precise."), they will learn that he packs "exactly" the same number of kernels in each bag of popcorn. This clue actually provides them with a synonym for *precise*, and will help them understand the meaning ("exact or accurate"). Encourage students to share other strategies they use when they encounter unknown words in their reading. Building word knowledge in this way nurtures inquisitiveness about language, promotes a broader vocabulary, and strengthens reading skills.

Name: _____     Date: _____

# Word Choice Chart

| Type of Word | What It Is | More Examples |
|---|---|---|
| Adjective | A word that describes a noun or pronoun, such as *excited*, *impressive*, *purple*, and *peculiar*. | |
| Adverb | A word that tells where, how, or when, such as *outside*, *carefully*, and *soon*. | |
| Exclamation | A word that expresses something, like surprise, anger, or pain. Examples are *Oh no!*, *Yeah!*, *Wow!*, and *Ugh!* | |
| Noun | A word that names a person, place, thing, or idea, such as *friend*, *city*, *skateboard*, and *friendship*. | |
| Plural Noun | A word that names more than one, such as *friends*, *cities*, *skateboards*, and *friendships*. | |
| Present-Tense Verb | A word that names an action, like *freeze*, *fly*, *sing*, and *sink*. | |
| Verb Ending in *-ing* | A word that tells what is happening, like *freezing*, *flying*, *singing*, and *sinking*. | |
| Past-Tense Verb | A word that tells what has already happened, like *froze*, *flew*, *sang* (or *sung*), *sank* (or *sunk*). | |

Name: _____     Date: _____

# The Fantastic
# Five-Step Process

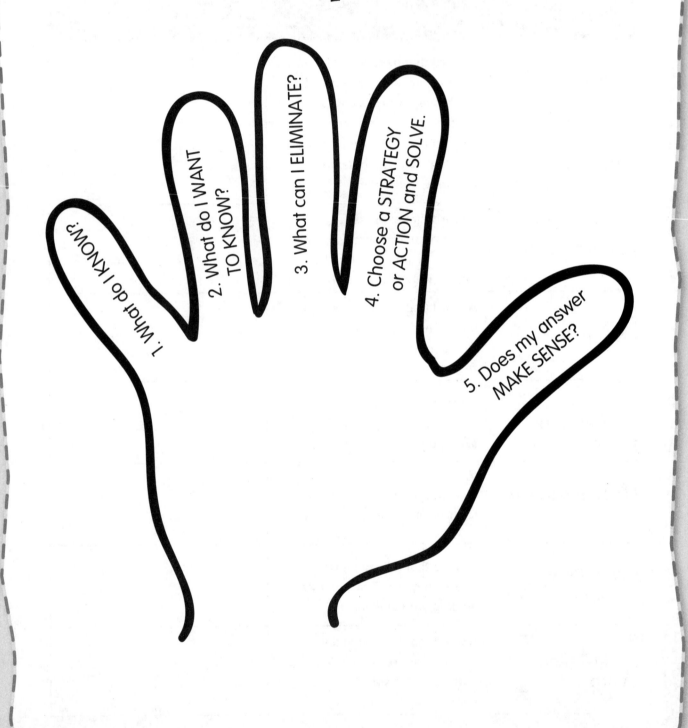

1. What do I KNOW?

2. What do I WANT TO KNOW?

3. What can I ELIMINATE?

4. Choose a STRATEGY or ACTION and SOLVE.

5. Does my answer MAKE SENSE?

**Identifying Fractions of a Whole**

# Giganto-Gum

**M**y _____
(choose a number: 2 or 3)

friends and I recently went to

_____'s Candy
(last name of a famous person)

Store. We usually go there to buy

comic books, _____, and candy. The store sells a new
(plural noun)

_____ gum called Giganto-Gum. One stick of it is
(adjective)

_____ inches long! It costs _____.
(number greater than 10)                                    (amount of money)

We pooled our money and bought one. Then we split up the gum

evenly. It tasted like _____ and smelled just like
(plural noun)

_____! We can't wait to get some more!
(plural noun)

How much Giganto-Gum
did each friend get?
Answer with a fraction. _____

Name: _____  Date: _____

# Baseball Team Championship

Our local baseball team, the

_____  _____
(name of a place)              (plural noun)

just won the league championship. Of _____
                                      (number between 6 and 19)

players, the two best are _____ and
                          (first and last name of a girl)

_____. This year the team won _____
(first and last name of a boy)                            (number greater than 1)

games. In the championship game they beat the _____
                                               (name of a place)

_____ by a score of _____ to 1. To help
(plural noun)                                   (number greater than 1)

celebrate, a local baker, _____, made a cake in the
                          (first and last name of a boy or girl)

shape of _____ Stadium. The cake was cut into as many
          (name of a place)

slices as players, so everyone got a piece.

How much of the cake
did each player get?
Answer with a fraction. _____

*50 Fill-In Math Word Problems: Fractions & Decimals: Grades 4–6 © 2009 by Bob Krech and Joan Novelli, Scholastic Teaching Resources*

Name: _____    Date: _____

# A New Candy

T he Really _____
                        (adjective)

Candy Company has just announced

the creation of their newest candy:

the _____-O Bar! It tastes just like
       (first name of a boy or girl)

_____, only chewy! It smells like a fresh,
       (plural noun)

yummy _____. Each bar is divided into
                    (noun)

_____ equal sections. _____
(choose one number: 4, 6, or 8)                    (first name of a boy or girl)

and _____ wanted to share one bar. They each chipped
       (first name of a boy or girl)

in _____ cents and bought one. They are saving it
       (number greater than 1)

for right after _____ practice. They know it will taste
                        (name of a sport)

_____, and they can't wait!
       (adjective)

**Solve This!** What fraction of the bar
should each person get? _____

Name: _____  Date: _____

# Bag of Marbles

**M**y brothers, _____,
(first name of a boy)

_____, and _____,
(first name of a boy)                                    (first name of a boy)

and I bought a bag of marbles. These are special marbles, made of

_____ instead of _____. Some are
(type of substance)                          (type of substance)

_____ and others are _____.
(color)                                       (color)

They roll well, but they also _____ remarkably well,
(present-tense verb)

too. There were _____ marbles in the bag, and we
(choose a number: 4, 8, or 12)

divided them evenly among us. Then we played _____
(name of a game)

with them. Marbles like this are valuable, so I am keeping mine in my

_____, where they will be safe
(type of furniture)

and _____.
(adjective)

**Solve This!**

What portion of the bag of
marbles did each brother get?
Answer with a fraction. _____

Name: _____  Date: _____

# Our Uncle's Popcorn

Our Uncle _____ is a great
(first name of a boy)

inventor. He invented the portable, electric _____.
(noun)

He also loves to invent new foods. Two of his best-known food inventions

are _____ spaghetti and _____
(noun)                                            (noun)

ice cream. His latest invention is _____ popcorn. Our
(noun)

uncle is very precise. He packs exactly _____ popcorn
(choose a number: 9, 12, or 15)

kernels in each mini-bag. Last night, my sisters, _____
(first name of a girl)

and _____, and I split a mini-bag evenly. The
(first name of a girl)

popcorn tasted very _____ and turned our tongues
(adjective)

_____! Our uncle says the next thing he is going to work
(color)

on is candy-coated _____. I can't wait!
(type of food)

**Solve This!**

How much of the mini-bag
did each person get?
Answer with a fraction. _____

Name: _____    Date: _____

# Our Garden

**M**y sister, _____,
(first name of a girl)

and I planted a garden. We are growing lots of

things, like _____,
(type of food)

_____, and _____
(type of food)                                    (adjective)

_____. We also grow vegetables. I grew a cucumber
(noun)

that was _____ inches long. My sister grew one identical to
(number greater than 1)

it. She cut her cucumber into _____ pieces. I cut
(single-digit number greater than 1)

my cucumber into _____ pieces. We each
(different single-digit number greater than 1)

gave our mother one of our pieces. She tasted them both and said,

"_____! These taste just like _____!"
(exclamation)                                              (plural noun)

Then she _____ all around the kitchen.
(verb ending in -ed)

---

**Solve This!**

How much of each cucumber,
expressed as a fraction, did
the children give their mom? _____

Who gave Mom the most? _____

---

Name: _____     Date: _____

# Building a Tree House

**M**y father and I are building a tree house.

It will have at least _____ windows
(number greater than 1)

and a roof made of the _____ we collected.
(plural noun)

We will climb up to it using a ladder made of special _____.
(plural noun)

To build the tree house, we needed wood and some _____ to
(plural noun)

hold the wood together. The wood was cut up into _____
(choose a number: 18, 20, or 24)

pieces. I took _____ pieces. My dad took
(single-digit number greater than 1)

_____ pieces. Then we got started. It only took
(different single-digit number greater than 1)

us _____ hours to put it together. We painted the tree house
(number greater than 1)

_____ and put a picture of a big _____
(color)                                                (noun)

on the side. It looks totally _____!
(adjective)

**Solve This!**

Use fractions to describe how much
wood each person got.

Father: _____     Child: _____

Name: _____     Date: _____

# Tunnel Discovery!

Two explorers found a mysterious tunnel known as the

Tunnel of _____. After _____
(last name of someone you know)                    (verb ending in -ing)

with shovels for _____ hours, they discovered an
(number greater than 1)

underground room filled with ancient _____. The
(plural noun)

explorers also found two bags filled with _____ coins.
(adjective)

The first bag had _____ coins, and the first
(double-digit number between 10 and 20)

explorer took _____ of these. The second bag had
(single-digit number greater than 1)

_____ coins, and the second explorer took
(different double-digit number between 10 and 20)

_____ of these. Both explorers were thrilled and used
(single-digit number greater than 1)

their coins to buy lots of _____.
(plural noun)

Use a fraction to describe what portion of the
coins each explorer took.

First explorer: _____     Second explorer: _____

Which explorer had more? _____

How do you know? _____

 *50 Fill-In Math Word Problems: Fractions & Decimals: Grades 4–6* © 2009 by Bob Krech and Joan Novelli, Scholastic Teaching Resources

Name: _____     Date: _____

# Diamond Rings

**S**ome of my relatives are very _____
(adjective)

and wealthy. My Great-Aunt _____ has a diamond
(first name of a girl)

ring. My Uncle _____ has a diamond ring, too.
(first name of a boy)

My great-aunt made all her money selling _____. Her
(plural noun)

ring has _____ stones in it, _____
(choose a number: 10, 12, or 14)          (single-digit number greater than 1)

of them diamonds. My uncle made a fortune when he invented

_____. My uncle's ring has _____
(plural noun)                              (choose a number: 10, 12, or 14)

stones in it, _____ of them diamonds. Both my
(single-digit number greater than 1)

great-aunt and my uncle are very _____. In fact, they
(adjective)

still like to _____ at the local bowling alley every week.
(present-tense verb)

---

**Solve This!**

Use a fraction to describe what portion
of the stones in each ring are diamonds.

Great-aunt's ring: _____     Uncle's ring: _____

Which ring has a greater
percentage of diamonds? _____

Name: _____ Date: _____

# Pizza Night

**O**n Friday night, we went to

_____'s Pizza Palace for dinner.
(last name of someone you know)

It is a very _____ place. The building is
(adjective)

shaped like a giant _____ and the waiters
(noun)

all dress like _____. I ordered the eight-slice
(type of occupation, plural)

_____ pizza. I ate _____pieces.
(type of food)                                    (single-digit number from 2 to 7)

My dad also ordered an eight-slice _____ pizza. He
(type of food)

ate _____ slices of his. Next time I have to try the
(single-digit number from 2 to 7)

_____ and _____ pizza. That
(type of food)                         (type of food)

sounds so _____!
(adjective)

---

**Solve This!**

What part of each pizza did they each eat?
Answer with a fraction.

Dad _____    Kid _____

How much of the pizzas did
they eat altogether? _____

Name: _____  Date: _____

# Our Chores

**M**y brother, _____, and I have chores to do every
(first name of a boy)

week. We each get paid _____ every week if we do our chores. I
(amount of money)

have to scrub the _____ with _____.
(noun)                                    (type of liquid)

My brother has to sweep the _____ and dust
(noun)

the _____. Of course, we also have to feed the
(noun)

_____. On Saturday, my mom asked us to wash a big
(type of animal)

window. It is _____ feet long and _____
(number greater than 1)                    (number greater than 1)

feet high. We divided the window into 20 sections. My brother washed

_____ sections. I washed _____
(single-digit number greater than 1)            (number from 2 to 18)

sections. I can't wait to get paid! I will be buying a big _____
(noun)

because I really want to _____ with it.
(present-tense verb)

How much of the window
did the kids wash altogether?
Answer with a fraction. _____

Name: _____  Date: _____

Addition With Fractions

# Short Book

**M**y name is _____
(first name of a boy)

and I have an amazing pet _____.
(type of animal)

In fact, I trained my pet to jump over _____.
(plural noun)

He can _____, _____, and
(present-tense verb)              (present-tense verb)

_____, too.  I know you won't believe this, but he can
(present-tense verb)

also write. He even wrote a book about _____.
(plural noun)

It's only ten pages, but it takes a while to read because the print is so tiny.

On Sunday, I read _____ pages. On Monday, I read
(choose a number: 2, 3, or 4)

_____ more pages. Now that he is famous, my pet is
(choose a number: 2, 3, or 4)

going to be on _____. For his appearance, he will be paid
(name of a television show)

_____ dollars!
(number greater than 1)

**Solve This!** How much of the book
did the boy read?
Answer with a fraction. _____

*50 Fill-In Math Word Problems: Fractions & Decimals: Grades 4–6* © 2009 by Bob Krech and Joan Novelli, Scholastic Teaching Resources

Name: _____    Date: _____

# After School

**A**fter school today I am going to walk to my

friend _____'s house. She
(first name of a girl)

lives on _____ Street, which
(noun)

is _____ tenths of a mile
(single-digit number greater than 1)

from my house and is right next to the Happy _____
(type of animal)

Restaurant. After we play _____, we are going to
(type of game)

_____'s house on _____
(first name of a girl)        (noun)

Avenue. That's another _____ tenths of a mile.
(single-digit number greater than 1)

She lives right behind _____ School. We can
(first and last name of a girl)

play on the _____ there and swing on the
(plural noun)

_____. It should be really _____!
(plural noun)                (adjective)

How far will the girl
have to walk after school?
Answer with a fraction. _____

Name: _____  Date: _____

# A Big Drink

**A** giant alien _____
(noun)

from the Planet _____ recently
(last name of a famous person)

landed in my backyard. He was actually very friendly and

_____. Since the trip was more than
(adjective)

_____ miles and it took _____ hours, he
(number greater than 1)                                      (number greater than 1)

was extremely thirsty. He gave me a recipe for his favorite drink. I got

a huge container. I filled _____ tenths of it with
(single-digit number greater than 1)

_____. Then I filled the rest of it with root beer. I shook it
(type of liquid)

up, put in a straw, and watched him drink the whole thing. Then he ate some

_____ topped with _____. Before
(plural noun)                                      (plural noun)

he left, he said it was the _____ snack he had ever had.
(adjective ending in -est)

**Solve This!** What part of the special
drink was root beer?
Answer with a fraction. _____

Name: _____  Date: _____

# Teeny-Tiny Plant-Growing Contest

**M**y friend _____ and I had a teeny-tiny
(first name of a boy)

plant-growing contest. I fed my plant _____. I
(plural noun)

even named it _____. My plant ended up being
(name of a famous person)

_____ tenths of an inch tall. My friend named his plant,
(single-digit number greater than 1)

too. He called it _____ _____.
(first name of a boy or girl)          (different name)

He watered his plant _____ times a day. His plant
(number greater than 1)

grew to be _____ tenths of an inch tall.
(different single-digit number greater than 1)

Both plants were _____ and beautiful. They had
(adjective)

_____ leaves and _____ stems. And
(color)                                    (color)

they smelled like _____!
(plural noun)

Which plant was tallest? _____

How much taller was it
than the other plant?
Answer with a fraction. _____

Name: _____  Date: _____

# New Fruit

D r. _____ is a famous
   (first and last name of a girl)

scientist in _____. She is especially
            (name of a place)

interested in studying _____
                      (plural noun)

and experimenting with fruit. She created a new fruit, which smells like

_____, is the size of _____, and tastes like
(type of fruit, plural)                  (type of fruit, plural)

_____. She gave me a serving that was _____
(type of fruit, plural)                                  (choose a number: 2 or 3)

fourths of the whole thing. I ate _____ eighths of that.
                                 (choose a number: 2 or 3)

It was _____. In fact, it made me want to
       (adjective)

_____ around the block! I can't wait for her next
(present-tense verb)

experiment. She is working on creating a new _____
                                             (noun)

that would be good for _____.
                      (verb ending in -ing)

**Solve This!** How much of the
serving was left?
Answer with a fraction. _____

Name: _____ Date: _____

# Birthday Cake

**M**y mother baked me an amazing

birthday cake for my _____
(ordinal number)

birthday. It looked just like a real _____ and had lots
(noun)

of decorations made out of _____-flavored icing. The
(type of food)

cake was cut up into ten pieces. My cousin _____
(first name of a boy)

ate _____ pieces. He wanted the pieces that had
(choose a number: 2, 3, or 4)

_____ on them. My sister, _____,
(plural noun)                                            (first name of a girl)

ate _____ pieces. She liked the pieces that had
(choose a number: 2, 3, or 4)

_____ on them. The cake was my favorite flavor,
(plural noun)

_____. Everybody sang _____ and
(noun)                                          (name of a song)

I blew out the _____. That was fun!
(plural noun)

How much of the cake was
left after the cousin and sister
took their pieces? Answer with a fraction. _____

*50 Fill-In Math Word Problems: Fractions & Decimals: Grades 4–6* © 2009 by Bob Krech and Joan Novelli, Scholastic Teaching Resources

Name: _____     Date: _____

# Road Race

The _____ Annual
          (ordinal number)

_____ Road Race
      (name of a place)

will take place this weekend. You have to run around the town of

_____  _____ times. Each lap
      (name of a town)        (single-digit number greater than 1)

around is _____ mile. You run as part of a team.
         (choose a number: $\frac{1}{4}$ , $\frac{1}{3}$ , or any other fraction)

My team is the _____  _____.
                    (adjective)                (plural noun)

The hard part is you have to carry two _____ and
                                              (plural noun)

pass them to a team member at the end of your lap. You also have to

wear _____ because the weather will most likely be
          (type of clothing)

_____. I am up for the challenge, though. I know
      (adjective)

I will _____  _____!
          (present-tense verb)        (adverb ending in –ly)

**Solve This!**   How many miles long
                  is the Road Race? _____

Name: _____    Date: _____

# Magic Show

_____,
(first name of a boy)

_____, and I went to a
(first name of a girl)

magic show at the _____ Theater.
(first and last name of a famous person)

_____ the Magnificent was performing. He was quite
(first name of a boy)

_____. First, he made his _____
(adjective)                                                                (noun)

disappear. Then he sawed a big _____ in
(noun)

half and even pulled some _____ out of my
(plural noun)

ear. At the end of the show he sold some of his special disappearing

powder. Each of us bought _____ of an ounce. I tried it
(any fraction)

on my _____. Sad to say, it did not work. I want my
(noun)

_____ back!
(amount of money)

**Solve This!** How much disappearing powder
did the three kids buy altogether? _____

_50 Fill-In Math Word Problems: Fractions & Decimals: Grades 4–6_ © 2009 by Bob Krech and Joan Novelli, Scholastic Teaching Resources

Name: _____     Date: _____

Multiplication With Fractions

# Favorite Cereal

_____ loves that
(first name of a girl)

new cereal, Frosted Mini-_____.
(plural noun)

What she likes most is that it is very _____ and
(adjective)

_____. _____ was having a sale
(adjective)                    (name of a store)

on her favorite cereal, so she bought _____ boxes.
(single-digit number greater than 1)

Each box was the _____-pound size. She told me
(choose a number: $\frac{1}{4}$ , $\frac{1}{3}$ , or any other fraction)

that sometimes she eats _____ bowls of this cereal a day.
(single-digit number greater than 1)

She likes it with _____ and _____
(plural noun)                        (plural noun)

on top. She says it tastes so _____this way!
(adjective)

I, myself, prefer _____ Pebbles because it is
(adjective)

so _____.
(adjective)

**Solve This!**

How much did the cereal the girl
bought weigh altogether? _____

 *50 Fill-In Math Word Problems: Fractions & Decimals: Grades 4–6* © 2009 by Bob Krech and Joan Novelli, Scholastic Teaching Resources

Name: _____          Date: _____

# Class Pet

**M**r._____'s
  (last name of a famous person)

students have a new class pet. It is a bit

unusual because it is from Planet

_____. We named it _____.
  (someone's last name)                              (first name of a famous person)

We have been feeding it _____ and giving it
                              (plural noun)

_____ to drink. This must be working well
  (type of liquid)

because our pet grew _____ of an inch every
                           (any fraction)

day for _____ days. It has turned a nice shade of
          (single-digit number greater than 1)

_____ and its hair is now about _____
  (color)                                            (number greater than 1)

inches long. I must say, it is really quite _____.
                                              (adjective)

**Solve This!** How much did the

class pet grow so far? _____

Name: _____          Date: _____

# Summer Camp

I went with my friend _____
(first name of a boy)

to a summer camp called Camp _____
(adjective)

_____. The camp leader, _____, was
(noun)                                    (name of a famous person)

at the entrance to welcome us. We get to do _____ stuff
(adjective)

like _____ and _____. We can swim
(present-tense verb)              (present-tense verb)

in _____ and hike across _____.
(body of water)                              (name of a place)

We were assigned to the _____ Patrol Tent. By the time
(type of animal)

we checked in, the tent was mostly full with other campers. There was only

_____ of the space left for us to sleep in. We split it up
(choose a number: $\frac{1}{2}$ , $\frac{1}{3}$ , or $\frac{1}{4}$ )

evenly though. I had plenty of room for my sleeping bag and my favorite

_____, as well as my bag of _____.
(noun)                                          (plural noun)

**Solve This!**

What fraction of the
remaining tent space did
each boy get for sleeping? _____

# Big Coconut

**F**our girls, _____,
(first name of a girl)

_____, _____,
(first name of a girl)                                  (first name of a girl)

and _____, recently went to the Island of
(first name of a girl)

_____. They enjoyed swimming in the fresh
(name of a store)

_____ pool and walking on the _____
(type of liquid)                                                      (color)

sandy beaches. They ate local food like grilled _____
(type of food)

and they cooled off with a local soda made from _____.
(type of fruit)

The hotel they stayed at gave them _____ of a coconut as a
(choose a number: $\frac{1}{8}$, $\frac{1}{4}$, or $\frac{1}{2}$)

welcome gift. They shared it evenly and ate it with _____
(type of substance)

sprinkled on top. That made it taste really _____!
(adjective)

**Solve This!**

How much of the coconut
did each girl get?
Answer with a fraction. _____

**Division With Fractions**

# Lawn-Cutting Service

**M**y friends and I started a lawn-cutting service.

What sets us apart from other lawn-cutting services

is that we use _____ and
(type of tool, plural)

_____ to get the job done.
(type of tool, plural)

We can cut a lawn in only _____ hours, which is
(number greater than 1)

impressive, don't you think? We even _____ the trees
(present-tense verb)

and shrubs. Recently, Mr. _____ asked us to cut half
(last name of a famous person)

his lawn. The _____ of us split the job evenly. When
(choose a number: 2, 4, or 8)

we were finished, the lawn looked _____. He paid us
(adjective)

_____ dollars each and gave us an ice-cold glass of
(number greater than 1)

_____.
(type of liquid)

**Solve This!**

How much of the lawn
did each friend cut?
Answer with a fraction. _____

Name: _____  Date: _____

# Grandma's Attic

**M**y brother, _____,
(first name of a boy)

and I were exploring our Grandma _____'s
(first name of a girl)

attic. We found old _____ and boxes of
(plural noun)

_____. There was even an old portrait of
(plural noun)

_____. We found a stuffed _____
(first and last name of a person)      (noun)

and a book written in _____. We also found
(year)

_____ of an ounce of gold! Grandma said we
(choose a number: $\frac{1}{16}$, $\frac{1}{8}$, $\frac{1}{4}$, or $\frac{1}{2}$)

could keep it if my brother and I shared it equally and promised not

to _____. I think I will use my part to buy a new
(present-tense verb)

_____. My brother says he is going to hide his in the
(noun)

_____. What a _____ day!
(noun)      (adjective)

---

**Solve This!**

What part of an ounce of
gold did each person get?
Answer with a fraction. _____

Name: _____     Date: _____

# Lab Report

**M**y science lab partner,

_____, and I had to do a
(first name of a girl)

report on _____. We researched the topic by going to
(plural noun)

_____, reading about _____, and
(name of a place)                              (plural noun)

watching some _____. So you know we learned a lot.
(plural noun)

I took notes with my _____. The report had to be ten pages
(noun)

long. My partner wrote _____ pages and I wrote the rest.
(single-digit number greater than 1)

When our teacher read our report, she said, "It's _____!"
(adjective)

She even _____ me on the back. We knew we did
(verb ending in -ed)

a really _____ job when we received a grade of
(adjective)

_____!
(number from 1 to 100)

**Solve This!**

How much of the report
did each partner write?
Answer with a decimal. _____

*50 Fill-In Math Word Problems: Fractions & Decimals: Grades 4–6* © 2009 by Bob Krech and Joan Novelli, Scholastic Teaching Resources

Name: _____     Date: _____

# Classroom Fix-Up

Our teacher, _____,
                    (name of a famous person)

decided it was time to fix up our classroom.

We all shared in the work. We started by

cleaning out all the old _____. Then we scrubbed
                                    (plural noun)

the floor with _____. We straightened our
                        (type of substance)

desks and _____ them. The room was looking
                    (verb ending in -ed)

_____, but we weren't finished yet. We divided one wall
            (adjective)

into ten sections. We bought _____ paint and started
                                            (color)

painting. We got _____ sections of the wall painted.
                        (single-digit number greater than 1)

It's going a little slowly because we have been _____
                                                            (verb ending in -ing)

at the same time, but we'll be finished soon. Our teacher says it should only

take another _____ days.
                        (number greater than 1)

**Solve This!**

How much of the wall was painted?
Answer with a decimal. _____

Name: _____     Date: _____

# Big Dance

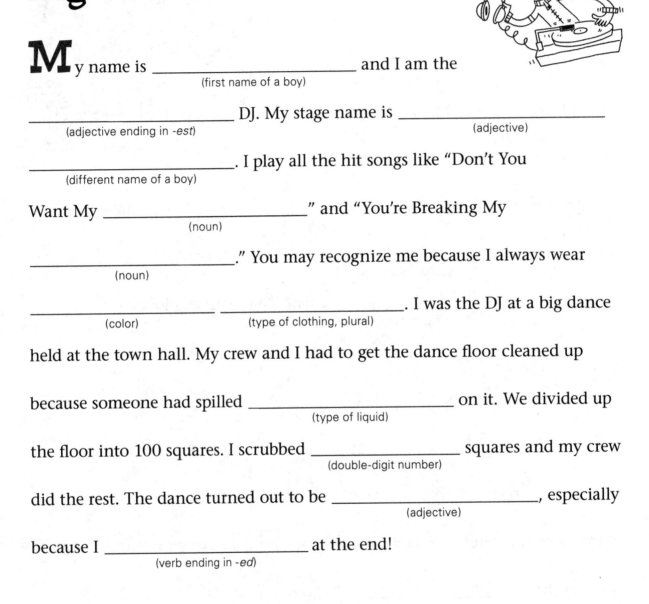

**M**y name is _____ and I am the
(first name of a boy)

_____ DJ. My stage name is _____
(adjective ending in -est)                                    (adjective)

_____. I play all the hit songs like "Don't You
(different name of a boy)

Want My _____" and "You're Breaking My
(noun)

_____." You may recognize me because I always wear
(noun)

_____ _____. I was the DJ at a big dance
(color)            (type of clothing, plural)

held at the town hall. My crew and I had to get the dance floor cleaned up

because someone had spilled _____ on it. We divided up
(type of liquid)

the floor into 100 squares. I scrubbed _____ squares and my crew
(double-digit number)

did the rest. The dance turned out to be _____, especially
(adjective)

because I _____ at the end!
(verb ending in -ed)

How much of the floor
did the DJ scrub?
Answer with a decimal. _____

Identifying Decimals

# Baseball Collectibles

**I** love collecting baseball stuff. I have

_____'s rookie card.
(first and last name of a boy or girl)

I even have a program from the first game that the

_____  _____
(name of a town)            (plural noun)

ever played. I just got my rarest baseball collectible ever. It cost

_____, but it was worth every cent. It is an original
(amount of money)

jersey worn by Babe _____. The thing is, it
(last name of someone you know)

was cut into a thousand pieces so that lots of collectors could purchase

a piece. I bought _____ of those pieces. I
(number from 2 to 99)

plan on putting them in a frame right next to my autographed photo

of Mickey _____, the greatest New York
(last name of a boy or girl)

_____ of all time!
(noun)

**Solve This!**  How much of the jersey
did the collector get?
Answer with a decimal. _____

Name: _____  Date: _____

# Card Game

**M**y cousin _____ and I
                (first name of a boy)

were playing a special card game we made up. It's called

_____ _____. To start, each player
        (adjective)                    (plural noun)

takes _____ cards. The players continue to pick cards until
       (single-digit number greater than 1)

they have _____ kings. The first player to get that many kings
           (number greater than 1)

wins! When my cousin and I played, the winner got part of a candy bar. The

candy bar had 10 sections. It was chocolate with _____
                                                        (type of substance)

filling. My cousin and I played the game two times. He won the first time, and

he got _____ pieces of the candy bar. I won the rest. The
        (single-digit number greater than 1)

candy bar was really _____, and I ate it right before I went
                            (adjective)

_____. Maybe that wasn't such a good idea.
       (verb ending in -ing)

**Solve This!**

How much candy did each player get?
Answer with decimals.

_____   _____

Name: _____    Date: _____

Comparing Decimals

# Big Football Team

**W**e have a really big football

team. In fact, we have a hundred

players. Of the players on the

team, _____ are
  (double-digit number)

girls. The rest are boys. The girls have _____ helmets
                                              (color)

and the boys have _____ helmets. We are called the
                        (color)

_____ - _____. Last week we
   (name of a town)         (plural noun)

played the _____ - _____. We
              (name of a town)         (plural noun)

won, _____ to _____. Our quarterback,
       (double-digit number)    (smaller double-digit number)

_____, threw _____ touchdown
   (name of a famous person)        (number greater than 1)

passes. It was the most _____ game ever!
                              (adjective)

**Solve This!** How much of the team is female? How much is
male? Use decimals to describe.

Female: _____    Male: _____

Name: _____    Date: _____

# Gumball Machine

As a special treat, my parents got me a gumball

machine. They gave it to me because I was so

_____. I _____ my room every day
(adjective)                          (verb ending in -ed)

and was always really _____ to my sister. The machine
                          (adjective)

was filled with gumballs. There were _____ green
                                        (single-digit number greater than 1)

gumballs and _____ red gumballs. There were some
                (double-digit number less than 80)

other colors, too, for a total of 100 gumballs in all. I know because I counted

them all. I chew my gum _____ times before I'm finished with
                          (number greater than 1)

it and I never stick it under the _____, like some people
                                    (noun)

do. When I'm finished, I always wrap my gum in _____
                                                  (plural noun)

and throw it in the _____, like you're supposed to do.
                      (type of container)

---

**Solve This!**

Use decimals to describe how much of each color
the gum was.

Green: _____  Red: _____  Other colors: _____

Name: _____     Date: _____

# Contest at the Fair

**I** went to the _____ County
                        (ordinal number)

Fair yesterday. There are rides there like the Haunted

_____ and the Tunnel of _____.
          (noun)                                         (plural noun)

There's lots of delicious food, too, like Cotton _____
                                                              (plural noun)

and Hot _____. But I was there to enter my
              (plural noun)

_____ in the Biggest Vegetable Contest. People call me
     (type of vegetable)

the Master Gardener, and the vegetable I entered shows why. It weighed

_____ ounces! My archrival, _____,
(decimal number greater than 1)                      (first name of a girl)

entered one that weighed _____ ounces. After the
                          (different decimal number greater than 1)

contest, though, we shook hands and shared a _____.
                                                  (type of beverage)

We even rode on the Spinning _____ together.
                                     (plural noun)

---

**Solve This!**

Whose vegetable weighed more? _____

By how much? _____
Answer with a decimal.

Name: _____     Date: _____

# Penny Collector

**M**y name is _____
(first name of a girl)

and I am collecting pennies to buy a new

_____ for my mom. I found _____
(noun)                                    (double-digit number less than 50)

pennies under the _____ and another
(noun)

_____ pennies in the _____.
(single-digit number greater than 1)          (noun)

Then I sold my _____ to my friend _____.
(noun)                                  (first name of a girl)

She gave me _____ pennies for it. Finally, I had enough
(single-digit number greater than 1)

money and I went to _____ and bought the gift.
(name of a store)

I wrapped it in _____ and gave it to my mother.
(plural noun)

When she saw it, she said, "_____!"
(exclamation)

**Solve This!**  How much money
did the girl collect?
Answer with a decimal. _____

Name: _____    Date: _____

# Fastest Man Alive

I am _____, the fastest
(first and last name of a boy)

person alive. I set a world record last week in the

_____    _____ run. It was two laps
(number greater than 0)        (distance unit, such as meter or yard)

around the track. I ran the first lap in _____ seconds. The
(decimal number)

second lap took me _____ seconds. That was a new world
(decimal number)

record! In order to run so fast I have to train hard. I do _____
(number greater than 1)

pushups every day and I run _____ miles every day, too. I
(number greater than 1)

make sure to eat plenty of _____ vegetables and drink
(adjective)

_____ glasses of _____ daily. In fact,
(number greater than 1)            (type of liquid)

I love training. Next week, I am going to start _____
(verb ending in -ing)

_____ times a day, too!
(number greater than 1)

**Solve This!** What was the new
world record time?
Answer with a decimal. _____

Name: _____   Date: _____

# Secret Recipe

**C**hef _____ won the
(first and last name of a girl)

_____ Cooking Contest today.
(name of a school)

She made her famous dish, Roasted _____.
(noun)

It is very _____ with a really _____
(adjective)                                    (adjective)

crust. The recipe is, of course, a secret. But we do know of one special

ingredient she added to the crust. She measured _____ounces
(decimal number)

of _____ and mixed it into the crust, and then
(type of substance)

added _____ ounces more. She stirred it with her favorite
(decimal number)

_____ for _____ minutes and then placed it in
(noun)                                (number greater than 1)

an ovenproof _____ to bake for _____ hours.
(noun)                                              (number greater than 1)

All of the judges had a taste, and said it was _____!
(adjective)

**Solve This!**   How much of the special
ingredient went into the crust?
Answer with a decimal. _____

Name: _____    Date: _____

# Clubhouse

**M**y friends _____
(first name of a boy or girl)

and _____ and I are building a
(first name of a boy or girl)

clubhouse in my yard for our club, the _____
(adjective)

_____. We named our clubhouse Fort _____.
(plural noun)                                                    (last name of a famous person)

We are building it out of _____ and _____.
(type of substance)                 (type of substance)

It has a room just for _____ and a space on the roof
(verb ending in -ing)

where we can _____. We put up a flagpole, too, which
(present-tense verb)

we made out of two sticks we joined together. One was _____
(decimal number)

meters long and the other was _____ meters long. Our flag
(decimal number)

has a beautiful _____ and _____
(color)                 (color)

_____ on it. That's our club mascot. I can't wait for our
(noun)

next meeting. We are going to _____ marshmallows!
(present-tense verb)

**Solve This!**

How long is the flagpole?

Answer with a decimal. _____

Name: _____     Date: _____

# Family Vacation

**M**y family went on a vacation to

_____. We drove
(name of a place)

there in our _____ _____, and it
(year)                        (type of animal)

took _____ days to get there. We did a lot of biking on our
(number greater than 1)

vacation. The first day we biked _____ miles. The second
(decimal number)

day we biked twice that. The third day we biked _____
(decimal number)

miles. We also swam in the _____ River. You have to
(last name of a boy or girl)

be careful because it is full of _____. We also saw
(plural noun)

the famous Mount _____ and bought souvenir
(last name of a famous person)

_____ and wore them everywhere. As you can see, it was
(plural noun)

a super-_____ trip!
(adjective)

**Solve This!**   How far did the family bike?
Answer with a decimal. _____

Name: _____   Date: _____

# Special Perfume

**M**y name is _____
(first name of a girl)

and I just got some of that popular designer

perfume, Summer _____.
(noun)

It is from the famous designer _____.
(first and last name of a boy)

It smells so _____, and it makes me feel like a
(adjective)

million _____. It cost me _____
(plural noun)                                         (number greater than 1)

dollars. I bought the _____-ounce bottle.
(decimal greater than 0.5)

I gave _____ ounces of it to my sister,
(decimal less than 0.5)

_____. She tried it on and said it smelled just like
(first name of a girl)

_____ _____. I will definitely
(adjective)                         (plural noun)

wear some the next time I go to _____!
(name of a place)

How much of the perfume did
the girl have left for herself?
Answer with a decimal. _____

Name: _____     Date: _____

# The Unusual Olympics

**I** am a member of the _____
(name of a place)

Team at the _____ Unusual Olympics. This year, it is being
(ordinal number)

held in _____ _____.
(adjective)                    (name of a place)

My time in the Race Around the _____ event was
(noun)

_____ minutes. I also did the _____
(number greater than 1)                        (noun)

Jump. My record in that event was _____ inches. In another
(decimal number)

event, the Grain of Salt Throw, my first throw was _____
(decimal greater than 0.5)

inches. My second throw went _____ inches. I won a
(decimal less than 0.5)

medal for the _____ Vault. The medal was shaped like a
(noun)

regular _____ and made of _____.
(noun)                              (type of substance)

I wear it around my _____ everywhere I go!
(body part)

---

**Solve This!**

How much farther was the first
throw than the second throw?
Answer with a decimal. _____

Name: _____     Date: _____

# Gigantic Snacks

**A** new restaurant called Gigantic Snacks just

opened up in _____. Everything
                    (name of a town)

on the menu here is enormous and nothing cost more than

_____! The first time I went, I had an amazingly
    (amount of money)

_____ hamburger that weighed _____
            (adjective)                                    (number greater than 1)

pounds. It came with a special _____-ounce
                                        (number greater than 1)

_____ milkshake that was so _____
            (flavor)                                          (adjective)

and creamy. I also got one French fry that was _____
                                                        (decimal greater than 0.5)

meters long! I dipped it in _____. It was delicious, but I
                                (type of condiment)

only ate _____ meters of it. I was so full, I sadly did not
            (decimal less than 0.5)

have room for their famous chocolate-covered _____.
                                                        (plural noun)

---

**Solve This!**   How much of the
French fry was left?
Answer with a decimal. _____

---

Name: _____    Date: _____

# School Store

**M**y name is _____ and
          (first name of a girl)

I want to tell you about my shopping experience at

our school store, the _____
                              (adjective)

_____. I had _____
(type of animal)              (double-digit number greater than 70)

cents. So I bought one _____ pencil that
                              (type of substance)

had a fun _____-shaped eraser. That cost
                    (noun)

_____ cents. I also bought a marker that smelled like
(number less than 20)

_____. That cost _____ cents. Finally,
(plural noun)                        (number less than 20)

I bought a cool, _____ _____
                         (adjective)                    (color)

notepad that was only _____ cents. I guess you could say
                              (number less than 10)

the school store is really _____!
                                    (adjective)

How much money did she have left?

Answer with a decimal. _____

Name: _____ Date: _____

# Candy Bar

**M**y friends _____
(first name of a boy)

and _____ and I went to
(first name of a girl)

the grand opening of _____'s Incredible Candy
(first name of a girl)

Emporium. There must have been _____ kids there! You could
(number greater than 1)

barely find a place to _____. We bought some Sour
(present-tense verb)

_____ and some Licorice _____.
(plural noun)                                          (plural noun)

But they were giving away pieces of a huge chocolate bar shaped like a fancy

_____. Each of us got _____ of
(noun)                                          (decimal less than 0.3)

the bar. It was so _____! I can't wait to go again next
(adjective)

weekend when they'll be giving away Fruity _____!
(plural noun)

**Solve This!**

How much of the bar did the
three friends get altogether?
Answer with a decimal. _____

Name: _____ Date: _____

# Special Drink

**M**y father said he was very thirsty after mowing

the lawn with our _____, so I made
                          (noun)

him a special drink. First, I got a large _____.
                                            (type of container)

I poured in _____ ounces of _____.
              (number greater than 1)                  (type of liquid)

Then I added _____ ounces of _____.
               (number greater than 1)                  (type of liquid)

I stirred it with the _____ and added some
                              (noun)

_____. To get the drink just right, I added
      (plural noun)

_____ ounces of water. That didn't quite do the trick,
    (decimal less than 0.3)

so I added the same amount _____ more times. I shook
                                (choose one: 2, 3, or 4)

it _____ times and then served it up. My father tasted it and
    (number greater than 1)

exclaimed, "This is positively _____!"
                                       (adjective)

How much water went
into the special drink?
Answer with a decimal. _____

Name: _____    Date: _____

# Do Your Chores

Last night, when I asked my

parents for an allowance, they said,

"_____, if you want to
<br>(first name of a girl)

be paid an allowance, you must do chores." So I have to

_____ my bed and dust my _____.
<br>(present-tense verb)                                    (noun)

I also have to scrub the _____ and take the
<br>(plural noun)

_____ out. I get paid _____
<br>(plural noun)                          (decimal number greater than 1.0)

dollars every time I do my chores. This month I did my chores a total of

_____ times. I put the allowance my parents gave me in my
<br>(choose a number: 2, 3, or 4)

_____, where it will be safe. I am saving up to get a motorized
<br>(type of container)

_____. I will ride it all over _____!
<br>(noun)                                         (name of a place)

**Solve This!** How much money
did the girl make this month?
Answer with a decimal. _____

Name: _____   Date: _____

# Class Poster

**I**n Mr. _____'s
(last name of a boy)

class we are studying _____.
(plural noun)

My group has to make a poster. We bought some

posterboard from _____'s Art Supply and
(last name of a famous person)

_____ Store. It cost $_____ per square
(noun)                                  (decimal less than 0.99)

inch. We bought _____ square inches. We drew with
(number greater than 1)

_____ and used _____ paint to
(plural noun)                        (adjective)

make it bright. We made a border out of _____ and stuck
(plural noun)

glow-in-the-dark _____ across the bottom. Everyone said,
(plural noun)

"_____!" when they saw it.
(exclamation)

How much did the
posterboard cost?
Answer with a decimal. _____

Name: _____    Date: _____

Division With Decimals

# School Carnival

_____,
(first name of a girl or boy)

_____,
(first name of a girl or boy)

_____, and I
(first name of a girl or boy)

were a team at our school carnival. It took place in _____.
(name of a place)

We did the _____ Toss together. We also did the
(noun)

_____ Relay together. Finally, our last event was
(noun)

_____ the Watermelon. Even though our team was
(verb ending in -ing)

_____, everyone said we were _____.
(adjective)                                              (adjective)

As a prize, the four of us got _____ of the
(choose a number: 0.125, 0.25, or 0.50)

watermelon to share among us, which is super because the only thing I like

eating better than watermelon is _____!
(plural noun)

Solve This!
How much of the whole watermelon
did each teammate get?
Answer with a decimal. _____

Name: _____    Date: _____

# Rare Mineral

**I** went exploring recently with

_____.
(name of a famous person)

We were digging around in _____'s
(first name of a boy or girl)

backyard, and were excited to find some _____ and even
(plural noun)

a few pieces of _____. But then we uncovered something
(noun)

truly amazing. It was a brilliant _____, it smelled like
(color)

_____, and it felt really _____! Yes!
(plural noun)                            (adjective)

It was that new, rare mineral, _____-anium! We found
(last name of a boy or girl)

_____ ounces in all, which the two of us
(choose a number: 0.10, 0.25, 0.50, 0.75, or 0.80)

agreed to split evenly. Now I think I'm going to be _____!
(adjective)

**Solve This!** How much of the rare mineral
will each explorer get?
Answer with a decimal. _____

Name: _____  Date: _____

# Odd Jobs

**S**ometimes my friends and I do

odd jobs around the neighborhood for

a little extra money. Last week we did

some jobs for Mr. _____. First we washed
                        (last name of a famous person)

his _____ and we cleaned all the trash out of the
          (noun)

_____. Then we raked his _____.
        (noun)                                        (noun)

We got paid _____ dollars, which the
              (choose a number: 0.20, 0.40, or 0.80)

_____ of us split evenly. You know we felt
  (choose a number: 2, 4, or 5)

_____! We split up the money, and started
        (adjective)

thinking about what we could do next. Maybe he'll pay us to paint the

_____ in his backyard!
        (noun)

How much money did
each person get?
Answer with a decimal. _____

Name: _____     Date: _____

# Snazzy Skis

I love skiing, especially on Mount

_____. To get ready for
(name of a place)

my ski trip there next week, I packed long _____
(type of clothing)

and warm _____. I asked my friend
(type of clothing)

_____ to help me get my skis ready by painting them!
(first name of a girl)

I wanted them to be _____, _____,
(color)                              (color)

and _____. I did one ski by myself and then we split the
(color)

painting on the other ski evenly. The ski is _____ meters
(decimal consisting of even digits)

long. It took us _____ to finish it because we painted a
(amount of time)

cool pattern of _____all over. Believe me, these skis look
(plural noun)

so _____, everyone will want to know where I got them!
(adjective)

How much of the ski did
each person paint?
Answer with a decimal. _____